Body Art

HAIR DECORATION

Paul Dowswell

www.heinemann.co.uk/library
Visit our website to find out more information about **Heinemann Library** books.

To order:
☎ Phone 44 (0) 1865 888066
📄 Send a fax to 44 (0) 1865 314091
💻 Visit the Heinemann Bookshop at www.heinemann.co.uk/library to browse our catalogue and order online.

First published in Great Britain by Heinemann Library, Halley Court, Jordan Hill, Oxford OX2 8EJ, part of Harcourt Education. Heinemann is a registered trademark of Harcourt Education Ltd.

Editorial: Lucy Thunder and Helen Cannons
Design: David Poole and Kamae Design
Illustrations: Kamae Design
Picture Research: Rebecca Sodergren and Elaine Willis
Production: Edward Moore

Originated by Repro Multi-Warna
Printed and bound in China by South China Printing Company
The paper used to print this book comes from sustainable resources.

ISBN 0 431 17925 5
08 07 06 05 04
10 9 8 7 6 5 4 3 2 1

British Library Cataloguing in Publication Data

Dowswell, Paul
Hair decoration. – (Body art)
391.5
A full catalogue record for this book is available from the British Library.

Acknowledgements

The Publishers would like to thank the following for permission to reproduce photographs:

Art Archive/Archaelogical Museum Bagdad/Dagli Orti p**9 top**; Bridgeman Art Archive p**22**; Bridgeman Art Archive/Giraudon p**26**; Bridgeman Art Library/Ali Meyer p**8**; Camera Press p**25 top**; Camera Press/Rajesh Bedi p**19**; Camera Press/A. Boot p**17**; Camera Press/Nick de Morgoli p**21**; Camera Press/Richard Stonehouse p**28**; Corbis/Earl & Nazima Kowall pp**18**, **20**; Corbis/Roger Ressmeyer p**4**; Getty Images/Imagebank p**29**; Hulton Archive p**12**; Imagestate p**6**; Mary Evans Picture Library pp**5**, **24**; Panos Pictures/Trygve Bolstad p**15**; Panos Pictures/Gianni Muratore p**23 top**; Rex Features pp**13**, **16**, **23 bottom**, **25 bottom**, **27 bottom**; Rex Features/Sipa Press p**11**; Science Photo Library p**27 top**; Still Pictures/Magnus Andersson p**14**; Topham Picturepoint p**7**; Werner Forman Archive p**9 bottom**; Werner Forman Archive/British Museum, London p**10**.

Cover photograph of a portrait of a punk, reproduced with permission of Getty Images/Photodisc.

The Publishers would like to thank Jenny Peck, curator at the Pitt Rivers Museum, University of Oxford, for her assistance in the preparation of this book.

Every effort has been made to contact copyright holders of any material reproduced in this book. Any omissions will be rectified in subsequent printings if notice is given to the publishers.

Disclaimer

Contents

Words appearing in bold, **like this**, are explained in the Glossary.

HAIR WORLD

'Like the clothes we wear, our haircuts say more about us that we would like to believe.' **Dylan Jones**, style journalist

The world of hair

Hair is an obvious and highly visible part of a person's appearance. From the very beginning of recorded history, hairstyles have been used to show that a person belongs to a particular group or has a certain **status** in society. The way a person wears their hair has a very personal element, too: it can allow them to express themselves, or simply make them feel good. Almost everyone wants to present themselves to the world with hair that flatters their face and gives them confidence.

In this book you can find out about the way hairstyles around the world have changed over time, and how what was popular hundreds or even thousands of years ago, comes around again.

Spreading trends

Until 500 or so years ago, the peoples of Europe, America, Africa and Asia would have had little if any contact with each other, and each developed their own distinctive hairstyles.

This Japanese punk rocker has dyed his naturally dark hair an outrageous pink, like punks from the 1970s and 80s did. Now young people take their hair fashions from all over the world.

In Europe, before the 20th century, kings, queens and the aristocracy usually set the scene for what was fashionable. **Archaeologists** have learnt that popular hairstyles in ancient Greece were illustrated in the painted figures on the side of their orange and black vases. What England's Queen Elizabeth I or Louis XIV of France wore in the 16th or 17th century would soon be copied by their courtiers. However, even for the rich and powerful, such trends took weeks or months to spread throughout the country. When fashions spread from court to court, from say Spain to Austria, the process could take months or even years. News of changing fashions generally concerned only the rich, and they would find out about any exciting new styles from portraits, or dolls.

Cutting hair

Hair is usually cut with scissors (known as shears in the hairdressing trade), or an electric cutter or razor. Each tool gives the hair a distinctive look. A razor cut, for example, tapers the hair, so it clings closely to the head. Scissors were invented around 1500BC. Before then hair was cut by a sharpened metal blade, or even a sharp flint stone. Ouch! This pair of scissors belonged to a woman during the Merovingian era in France (c. AD 450 to 750).

Hair today

Today, trends and styles spread easily and quickly. We can see David Beckham's latest hair cut, for instance, almost as soon as it has been finished. Following the great age of exploration and massive human **migration** from one part of the world to another, there is much greater knowledge and interest in the fashions and styles of other cultures, too. At the start of the 21st century, all around us, we can see a mind-boggling variety of styles, colours and cuts taking their inspiration from every time and culture known to humankind. And we can experiment with dyeing, perming, threading or braiding like never before.

Hollywood child actress Shirley Temple, popular in the 1930s, holds a doll displaying her much-imitated curly ringlets.

Hair and who you are

Clues to identity

Throughout history, and everywhere on Earth, hairstyles have been used to show that a person belongs to a particular social group. Even today, from a judge's wig to the shaven logo hip-hop hairstyles of pop stars, what people do with their hair sends a message to those around them. There is no getting away from it – even if you have the most anonymous or old-fashioned haircut, you are still announcing: 'I don't care about fashion' – which is fairly remarkable these days. Your hair can not only indicate your social **status**, it can show what sort of job you do, what sort of religion you are and even what sort of music you like. In some cultures, by marking a **rite of passage**, a hairstyle can also show what stage of life you are at.

First impressions

Your face and hairstyle are invariably the first things someone else notices about you. Our assumptions about hairstyles are so strong that many people will jump to conclusions about an individual based on that style.

We tend to think that a hairstyle can say a lot about what sort of job someone does; for instance, we often associate short, tidy men's haircuts with office work. All sorts of jobs where the person has to meet or serve the general public, such as airline pilots, police or bank workers, demand that employees have groomed, tidy hairstyles. Professions such as sport and popular music allow people much more scope for expressing themselves through imaginative and daring hairstyles.

Hair to remember

In Victorian England, when a person died, a lock of their hair was taken to remember them by. Sometimes this hair would be woven into strands to make up special **mourning** jewellery. Sometimes, this could be in the shape of a bow or flower.

Styles can easily be inspired by fashion, and may or may not signify a person's opinions or beliefs. Some hairstyles, though, do – the monk's **tonsure** or the distinctive **sidelocks** or beard and skull-cap of the **Orthodox Jewish** man, both send a clear message about the wearer's religious convictions.

This Australian snowboarder is copying the floppy hair of the American snow and skate boarders who first took up these sports.

> 'Hair has no practical use other than to make a personal, tribal or class statement.' **Ted Polhemus**, social historian

Fashion parade

Particular hairstyles do not only set certain groups of people apart from the rest of society, they also offer a clear visual signal to other like-minded individuals. This can be seen today, for example, in the various types of youth culture. Surfers, skateboarders, snowboarders, grunge and Indie fans all have distinct hairstyles that advertise their musical and lifestyle choices. Such styles are often set by musical and sporting heroes, and fans are constantly updated on the latest looks by magazine and newspaper features.

These US Marines all sport the regulation shaven-headed style required by their particular branch of the military.

Identity parade

In previous centuries, soldiers and sailors wore wigs or had longer hair, but significantly, the style of the hair or wig was identical for each particular regiment. In the 18th century, the Royal East Kent Regiment wore **buff** coloured wigs, and the Royal Horse Guards wore blue coloured wigs. Even today, these regiments are still known as the 'Buffs' and the 'Blues', although they no longer, of course, wear wigs. In the 19th century, British soldiers were required to wear moustaches. Young soldiers, who were yet to grow hair on their face, had to paint on a moustache! Although it sounds a bit ridiculous to us, it was important as it encouraged comradeship and loyalty. It also helped to avoid mistaken identity in the panic and horror of hand-to-hand fighting.

GET THAT HAIR CUT!

In many countries in the world, men in the armed forces have short hair. Having the same haircut and wearing the same uniform takes away a person's sense of individuality. Accepting the short haircut shows that the new **recruit** also accepts the strict discipline of army life. This has a **psychological** effect: all the recruits have the same haircut, so no one stands out – their hair is one thing they all have in common. This makes it easier for them to feel part of their fighting unit.

Hair in early human history

Early clues

Among the earliest evidence of human art and culture, such as the first patterns etched on pots and the first jewellery, are the first clues to early human hairstyles. The very first hairstyle we know of appears on the ample figure of a limestone carving of a woman known as the 'Willendorf Venus' – after the area in which it was discovered in Austria. This dates from around 25,000 BC. The carving had probably been used in early religious rituals. Although the head of the carving does not show facial features, it clearly shows an intricately arranged, braided and layered hairstyle. Whoever wore this hairstyle at the time must have taken hours of careful work to prepare their hair.

Civilized curls

Civilizations from the Persian Gulf in the Middle East, such as the Sumerians (4000 BC to 3000 BC) and the Babylonians (2000 BC to 500 BC), left evidence of quite distinct and complex hairstyles. Carved stone statues, **figurines** and wall **reliefs**, show both men and women favoured curls. Most Sumerian noblewomen are shown with hair dressed in a heavy, netted knot at the back of the head, or in rolls and plaits. Hair was also allowed to fall over the shoulders in a plain, simple style. Women of lower **status** have been shown wearing this style, sometimes with a simple wood or fabric hair band to hold the hair away from the face. From the evidence that remains, **archaeologists** suggest that people who did not have naturally curly hair would have used heated metal curling tongs. Statues of rulers from this period show that elaborate curled beards were also fashionable. Hair could be dyed with mineral **pigments** from the earth, such as ochre (with shades of red through to yellow), and pyrolusite (black).

The Willendorf Venus dates from around 25,000 BC, and is the first archaeological evidence of human hairstyling. These intricate braids and layers must have taken many hours of careful preparation.

Time is money

Those with power and wealth were keen to display hairstyles which required a great deal of attention and upkeep. This sent a clear message that they had both the time to be pampered, and the wealth to afford servants or slaves to do the pampering. Interestingly, the **visual records** of these early civilizations show that many of those who did basic work, such as labouring in the fields, had shaven heads. Even as the first societies and cities sprang up, a clear link was emerging between hair and status. Six or seven thousand years later, an elaborate and expensive cut stills sends out a message – 'I have the time and the money to afford a hairstyle like this'.

FACT

Wealthy Sumerian men and women would sometimes sprinkle their hair with gold dust, to make it glitter in the light.

This Sumerian statue from c.3000 BC depicts a wealthy man who shows his style and status by curling his hair and beard. Wealthy Sumerian women also had intricately fashioned hair.

EARLY HAIR ACCESSORIES

The first evidence of hair ornaments survived from this early period of human civilization (4000 BC onwards). Combs, hair slides, grips and other implements to hold hair in place have been found at burial and settlement sites. These hair accessories were often carved from ivory or bone or forged from gold and silver, then carved with intricate patterns. Our modern plastic equivalents are still remarkably similar in design. The care and attention needed to make them tell us that the people that produced them thought their appearance was very important. Hair accessories were used to show both people's status and enhance their appearance. This ivory hair comb comes from Egypt and dates from c.3000 BC.

EGYPT, GREECE AND ROME

Ancient Egypt

During the time of the Ancient Egyptians (around 3000 BC to 30 BC) a person wore a hairstyle that showed everyone around them how important they were. Kings, priests and **aristocrats** all had distinctive hairstyles and beards. The Egyptian Queen Hatshepsut even wore a false chin beard when she appeared in public, as beards were an important symbol of royal authority! Laws were created which banned ordinary people from wearing particular hairstyles.

The highest-ranking Egyptians usually shaved their heads and wore wigs of real human hair. These were often braided and woven with golden tubes or other ornaments. In the hot Egyptian climate, having a shaven head kept you cool and protected you from head lice. Wigs also disguised deformities and made hair look thicker, which was considered attractive, as it still is now. Less expensive wigs were made of a mixture of human hair and strands of vegetable fibre. We know a lot about Egyptian wigs because many have been found in tombs. They were carefully looked after with **emollients**, oils, scented petals and even chips of fragrant wood, such as cinnamon. Peasants and ordinary towns' people had to make do with their own hair.

This wall painting shows a wealthy Egyptian woman wearing an elaborate hairstyle. Although we cannot be sure, the hair is almost certainly a wig worn over a shaven head. The cone on her head is made of oils which would have melted to keep her cool.

EGYPTIAN HAIR CARE

The ancient Egyptians worried about going grey just as people do today. A dark mixture of black cow blood, black snake fat and raven's eggs was said to restore hair to a luscious black sheen. Modern colour restoring products, such as *Grecian 2000*, and *Youthair®*, are creme or liquid solutions manufactured from a list of carefully chosen chemicals. Look on the ingredients and you might see chemicals like propylene glycol, ceteareth-20, sulphur and acetic acid.

Greece and Rome

Fashions came and went in ancient Greece and Rome (roughly 800 BC to AD 450), just as they do today. For men, short hair or shaggy hair, a beard or a clean-shaven face all came in and out of fashion. For women, hair piled on top of the head, tied with a scarf or held in place with a tiara, were all popular styles at one time or another. Generally, in both these cultures, short hair was usually in fashion for men. We know about these styles because they were shown on decorated pots, wall paintings, statues, **friezes**, **mosaics** and other **visual records**.

In ancient Rome, the conquests of the Roman army brought lots of slaves from northern Europe. Rich Romans, bored with their dark Mediterranean hair, might shave the heads of blonde Anglo-Saxon or Germanic slaves and use the hair to make wigs. Poor Romans with beautiful hair would also sell it to wig makers. Both Roman men and women used hair dyes – the reddish tint of **henna** was particularly popular. Hair dyes were unreliable though, and could produce disastrous results. The Roman poet Ovid wrote a very cross letter to his girlfriend saying, 'Didn't I tell you to stop messing around with the colour of your hair? Now you have no hair left to dye!'

FACT

Julius Caesar used to have his facial hair plucked out with tweezers.

Russell Crowe plays Roman general Maximus Decimus Meridius in the film Gladiator. His cropped hairstyle and closely-shaved beard was typical of that worn by men from ancient Rome. It was designed to make a clear statement of their own clean-living civilization, compared to the straggly beards and long hair of their Barbarian enemies.

STONE HAIR

During Roman times, wealthy women would commission a sculptor to carve them as a marble **bust**. Because hair fashions changed so frequently, they often requested that the hair part of the head should be detachable, so that their latest style could be placed on the bust.

BEARDS

'A beard covers a multitude of chins.' **Anon**

Attitudes to beards

Like hairstyles, beards have been in and out of fashion since the dawn of recorded history. The ancient Greeks and Romans saw a clean-shaven face or a short, well-groomed beard as a mark of civilization. In ancient Greece only **Spartan** warriors sported full beards until Alexander the Great (356 BC to 323 BC) ruled that all soldiers were to shave to prevent their beards being grabbed in battle.

> ### BEARDS AND BELIEFS
>
> In some religions, such as for **Sikhism** and **Orthodox Judaism**, beards on men are worn as a symbol of their religious belief. Hindu men from Rajasthan in India wear an elaborate curled moustache and a full beard to show their devotion to the **Hindu** religion. Beards can also be used to show political beliefs. In Italy in the 1920s and 1930s, many followers of Benito Mussolini's **Fascist** party wore the 'Balbo' beard, neatly trimmed under the chin with a separate moustache and clean-shaven cheeks. The beard was named after a leading Fascist, Italo Balbo, who sported such a beard.

Beards can also arouse strong feelings. 'Never trust a man with a beard – they've got something to hide', used to be a common saying. The Russian **Tsar**, Peter the Great (1672–1725), was keen to modernize and update his society. He banned beards because he saw them as symbols of an old-fashioned attitude. This was so unpopular he had to back down, but introduced a tax on beards instead.

Psychologist Robert J. Pellegrini once said 'the male beard communicates an heroic image of the independent, sturdy, and resourceful pioneer, ready, willing and able to do manly things.' As a general rule, beards have usually been regarded as a badge of masculinity. But curiously, this has not always been the case. In late Victorian and Edwardian Britain, for example, beards dropped out of favour. Their association with 19th century artists led them to be considered **effeminate**!

Count Italo Balbo (1896–1940) was a leading Fascist in Mussolini's Italy. His distinctive facial hair was much imitated in that country during the 1920s and 1930s.

Pop and fashion icon George Michael models one of the 1980s most distinctive looks – 'designer stubble'. This almost beard required skilful maintenance with a special trimming tool, to keep it just the right length.

Further out of fashion

In Europe, Australia and North America, beards virtually vanished between World War I and the 1950s. During this time, fashion-conscious young people took their cue from beardless movie stars. But in the 1950s young men showed their loyalty to the emerging '**Beatnik**' culture by sporting a goatee beard, which covered the top lip and chin. In the 1960s, **hippies** grew long, luxurious beards to show their disrespect for the rules and regulations of society. In the go-getting 1980s, men often sported a short beard in a style known as 'designer stubble'. Made popular by celebrities such as George Michael, it became an acceptable look. It was even accepted in professions such as banking and insurance, where an unshaven, stubbly face would usually be frowned on as a sign of personal untidiness.

Today's beards

Today, beards are no longer associated with unruly, antisocial behaviour, but can still be a symbol of rebellion in some quarters. Some **anti-establishment** bands sport fashionable goatees; goatees made a comeback among pop musicians in the grunge era of the early 1990s and nu-metal style of the early 21st century.

'He that hath a beard is more than a youth, and he that hath no beard is less than a man.' **William Shakespeare**, *Much Ado about Nothing*, Act II, Sc. 1

AFRICA

Plaits to petals

Africa is a continent with an extraordinary mixture of different cultures, so it is not surprising to learn there are a huge range of hairstyles found there. Many Moroccan women, for example, arrange their hair in long thin plaits. Women of the Peul people of the Fouta Djallon in Guinea make large, petal-shaped **braids**, with hair splayed out to fill in the gap. Male Masai warriors have a complex style of long braided hair in up to 400 strands, arranged in pigtails and tied with sheepskin. Arranging a style like this can take up to 20 hours.

As in other cultures and continents, hairstyles are often closely tied to an individual's place in a society and they can mark a **rite of passage**. In some cultures a female will have a distinctive hair cut at every stage of her life – whether she is an unmarried girl, a married woman, a mother or a widow. Bangwa women from western Cameroon shave their hair when they marry, but a mother of twins is allowed to grow her hair long.

Celebratory style

In some parts of Africa, hairstyles are worn as a celebration. Hamar youths of southern Ethiopia, for example, construct a most elaborate hairstyle, called a '*boro*', to mark the planting of crops, or a successful hunt. This complex hairstyle is usually created with the help of a friend or partner. Hair is trimmed and plaited, then clay is smoothed over part of the head. Feathers are added as an additional decoration. Senior members of the Hamar tribe can demand especially fine feathers from the heads of younger members.

The Mangetu tribe

Perhaps most striking of all are the hairstyles worn by women of the Mangbetu tribe of Zaire. The Mangbetu consider an elongated skull to be beautiful, and babies have their heads bound in hide or bark cloth to encourage them to grow in this way. Hair on the head is braided tightly to the skull, and at the crown is woven with straw and hair ornaments to make a disc shape. This helps to further exaggerate the elongated shape of the head.

This Samburu man is a warrior (known as a moran). The moran braid their hair and cover it in the red dye ochre. They stop doing this when they reach their late teens or early twenties.

FACT
....
Hamar women have their own distinctive hairstyle. They roll strands of their hair in ochre, butter and acacia gum. This gives an effect which resembles locks of tightly braided hair.
....

Hair threading originated in Western Africa, and has been popular in that continent for centuries. The style is referred to as an Onigi design – a Yoruba word meaning sticks. The hair is gathered up into tight strands and held in place by thread.

Cornrows and threads

Two styles common all over the continent, but originating in West Africa, are cornrowing and threading. In cornrowing, the hair is plaited tightly against the scalp to form patterns in the lines between the plaits. Beads or other ornaments can also be woven into the hair. In threading, locks of hair are wrapped in thread, to create three-dimensional styles of raised strands (see panel). These styles have become popular all over the world.

THREADING YOUR HAIR

If you want to try out this popular West African style, you will need a comb, scissors, thread the same colour as your hair and some hair oil:

- Comb your hair out straight and divide it into sixteen or so strands.
- Tie each strand together with a clip or elastic band.
- Take a strand, remove the clip and twist the hair with oil.
- Take a metre of doubled thread and twist it round the strand. You need to begin at the bottom, next to the scalp, and twist up to the top.
- Tie a knot in the thread two or three times at the tip of the hair, and cut off the loose thread ends.
- Carry on, one section at a time, until you have finished.

BLACK HAIR

Black hair across the world

Black people live all over the world and styles that originated in Africa have travelled to many places with the **migration** of people. For example, distinctive cuts worn by well-known black performers in the global music industry have helped to spread black hairstyles across the world. They are then adopted by other people and cultures.

The Afro

The Afro, or 'fro' is a hairstyle where curly hair grows out in a soft ball around the head. People of African origin have several different types of hair, but most will be familiar with the downy, curly, frizzy hair that can grow into an Afro. This type of hair is often referred to as 'nappy' hair. If it is left to grow naturally without any perms (permanent hair treatments) or **relaxers** to straighten it out, it can be teased into an amazing gravity-defying hairstyle.

Contemporary American singer Macy Gray models a hairstyle popular three decades previously. Already tall, her Afro adds further inches to her height, making her seem even more larger than life. She is an example of how the nappy Afro can look fantastic.

HOW TO GET THE AFRO LOOK

Massage a little moisturizing oil into your hair. Then take a pick or small comb and lift the hair until it stands on end. It is best to start at the ends of your hair and work down to the roots – this will stop it from breaking and it will be less painful getting knots out. To finish it off, pat the Afro into a neat, rounded shape.

Dreadlocks

Along with braids and threading, one of the most common black hair styles is dreadlocks. Here, hair is grown into long matted strands which are left uncombed. The present fashion for the style first originated in Jamaica in the 1930s. Dreadlocks are now seen all over North America and Europe, and are also popular in African countries such as Ghana, Tanzania and Zimbabwe.

The dreadlock style was originally worn by Rastafarians – a religious sect from Jamaica. They believe the Ethiopian king Haile Selassie (1892–1975) is God – and wear dreadlocks as a symbol of their religion.

This instantly recognizable style was made popular by international reggae superstar and Rastafarian Bob Marley, and other Jamaican reggae musicians. The origin of the style has several explanations. One is that it is in imitation of the hairstyle worn by Ethiopian tribal warriors, who, in turn, cultivated their hair in imitation of the mane of a lion. Another explanation is that the style is inspired by a passage in the Bible, from Numbers 6:5. It reads, 'there shall no razor come upon his head … he shall be holy, and shall let the locks of the hair of his head grow.' Not everyone who has dreadlocks is a Rastafarian of course – it is also a fashion statement and hairstyle.

Black hair today

Today, modern hair-care technology allows people to almost completely change the length, thickness, colour, texture and style of their hair whenever they choose. This is especially appealing to celebrities. The pop group Destiny's Child, for example, model an amazing collection of different hairstyles, making use of techniques such as colouring, curling, straightening and **hair extensions**. So Beyoncé Knowles, for example, can swap her braids for long blond, ringlets and Kelly Rowland can wear her hair in a short, straight bob.

FACT

Dreadlocks are so called because they are meant to inspire dread – fear – in the enemies of Rastafarianism.

The international success of reggae star Bob Marley in the late 1970s popularised both his distinctive dreadlock hairstyle and the Rastafarian religion.

HAIR AND RELIGION

Visible differences

A distinctive hairstyle or lack of hair can be used to symbolize the wearer's religious beliefs. Different religions have cultivated their own specific hairstyles and traditions which separate them from others. **Sikh** men, for example, do not shave. Neither do they cut their hair. Instead, they wrap it inside a **turban**. Some **Hindu** holy men, on the other hand, shave the head to symbolize their rejection of bodily and worldly pollution. From birth, a Hindu boy's hair is left uncut until he becomes an adult. Then it is cut and given as an offering at the shrine of a god. **Hare Krishna** converts shave their heads to show their commitment to their belief. **Islam** has a tradition of covering the head and hair with a turban, head-cloth or **fez** for men, and a shawl for women. In some Islamic cultures, women keep their entire head covered in public, showing no evidence of hair at all.

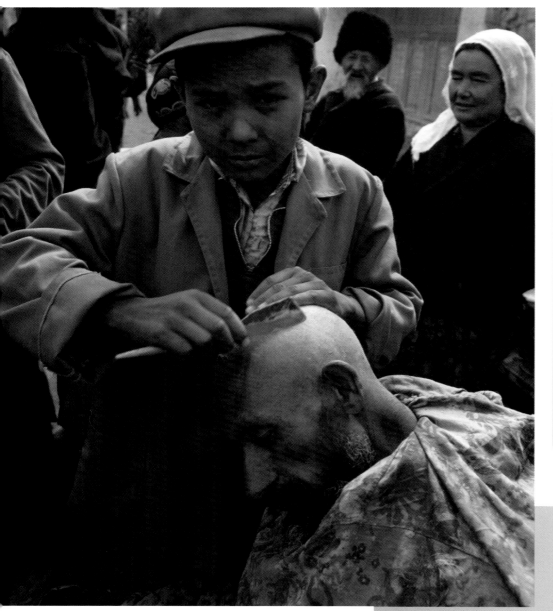

HIDING HAIR

Throughout history, and in many different cultures, hair has been considered a central part of what makes a woman beautiful. Strict rules have developed, mostly based on religious ideas, about the display of a woman's hair. Today, many Islamic people believe that it is wrong for a woman to show her hair in public. In the Middle Ages (roughly 900–1500) in Europe, the Christian church encouraged women to hide their long hair in a wimple. Nuns were required to shave their hair off altogether. Jewish women may also face severe disapproval if they untie their hair or leave it uncovered.

This teenage barber is shaving the head of a Muslim man in prepartion for Friday prayers in Karghalik, Xinjiang Province, China.

His head shaven in an act of symbolic purification, this Hindu man is bathing in the sacred Ganges River, which runs through the city of Varanasi in Northern India. Hindu pilgrims come to Varanasi from all over the world to bathe in the Ganges. They believe that it will cleanse them of their sins.

Loyalty to traditions

A commitment to a religious belief, as shown in a style of hair, is important to people throughout the world. The Amish are a branch of the Christian faith who live in Pennsylvania, Ohio, and other parts of North America. They value simplicity in their lifestyle and this is reflected in their distinctive hairstyles. Amish men wear their hair cut short, evenly all around the head, to just below the ear, or above the earlobe. This was a common style among men in the 18th century, when the Amish first came to America from Europe. Amish women are expected to wear their hair long and uncut, parted down the middle, and covered with a bonnet. Amish girls have their hair **braided** from the time they are babies until they reach adolescence.

HAJJ

The Hajj is a holy journey or pilgrimage, which **Muslims** are supposed to make at least once in their lifetimes. They travel to Makkah and take part in the Hajj. Completing the Hajj is like having your slate wiped clean – all your sins have been wiped out and you can start afresh. As a symbol of this, Muslim men will have all their hair shaved off before they go. Muslim women usually only cut off a lock of hair as a symbolic 'shaving'.

CHINA AND JAPAN

Chinese traditions

The history of hairstyles in the great eastern cultures of China and Japan seems almost unchanging. In China, during the Qing **dynasty** (1644–1911), the Manchu Emperors forced the men in the Chinese regions they ruled over to wear a Manchu-style pigtail. This was a sign of the men's submission to the dynasty. Generally, women in China were expected to grow their hair long, but keep it in a neat bun on the back of their head, or two coiled buns on the sides of their head. Right up until the 20th century it was considered improper for Chinese women to wear anything other than a traditional hairstyle.

There were differences in styles in such a large country as China. In Xinjiang, for example, women wore their hair in long ponytails, interwoven with elaborate coins, beads and other ornaments. This style can still be seen today.

Revolution

As China grew more open to outside influences, some daring women, notably actresses, began to cut their hair in a shorter style. Then, during the upheaval of the Civil War and Revolution (1927–49), many women wore their hair cut short because it was difficult to keep long hair clean and cared for in those troubled times. The years that followed under the rule of the Chinese **Communist regime** were repressive (restraining). The regime had strict ideals, which discouraged Western hairstyles, declaring them **decadent**. So, shorter hair remained common, as did two neat braided pigtails.

Now, at the start of the 21st century, China is again more open to outside influence, and Chinese men and women wear their hair in whatever style they choose.

This Tajik woman of Xinjiang Province, China, wears her hair in a style traditional to the area. The large white buttons among the braids signify that she is married.

Japanese styles

The Japanese only welcomed Westerners to their country in the middle of the 19th century. Before then, Japanese hairstyles for men had favoured a combination of a shaved forehead and a pigtail at the back of the head. Japanese warlords would shave or pluck the hair from the front of their hairline to make their foreheads look higher. High-class women's styles were a complex arrangement of hair piled high and held in place with chopstick-like rods. Japanese **geishas** traditionally wore stiff black wigs when in ceremonial costume. During the second half of the 19th century, Japan transformed itself into an industrial nation, and many Japanese took to wearing their hair in short European and American cuts to show their enthusiasm for this new modern Japan.

NECK AND NECK

The Japanese style of piling hair high on the head is intended to show off the nape of the neck – an area of the body Japanese find especially beautiful. This style was briefly popular in late 19th century Paris, which looked to the rest of the world for fashion inspiration.

FACT

In northern Japan, women of the Ainu people are tattooed with a moustache when they get married.

GEISHA HAIR

The distinctive geisha hairstyle takes at least a couple of hours to perfect. To keep the style in prime condition, a geisha needs to visit a hairdresser once a week. She also has to sleep on a wooden block instead of a pillow to keep her hair in place. To achieve the look, sections of the hair are oiled and waxed, before being pinned in place. Then, extensions are used to thicken the geisha's real hair. The constant pulling and tugging to achieve this style can cause bald patches.

This geisha has an intricate bun and hair ornaments as part of her hairstyle. This style is applied with great care and patience, and dates back many centuries.

THE AMERICAS

Sketchy impressions

Our knowledge of North and South America before the arrival of Europeans in the late 15th century is sketchy. Few of the many peoples of these two vast territories kept written records. But when European settlers arrived in these lands they did record their impressions of the lifestyles and appearance of the people they met.

Life stages

In North America there are many different **indigenous** peoples, cultures and traditions. There is also a huge variety of **Native American** hair – it can be straight, wavy and even curly, and many hair colours can be found among Native Americans.

A common traditional style for men and women is to wear their hair long and parted in the middle. It can be held in place with a headband, or worn in two plaits either side of the head. Braiding is also practised, as is the weaving of beads, bone piping and feathers into the hair. Men, as a rule, do not grow beards, preferring to pluck or **singe** their facial hair. Head hair used to be held in place with buffalo grease. As with many other cultures, hairstyle can be used to symbolize a particular stage in life. For girls of the Hopi people, for example, it is traditional to wear their hair in a distinctive style piled high on the head, until they get married. Then, they can wear their hair down.

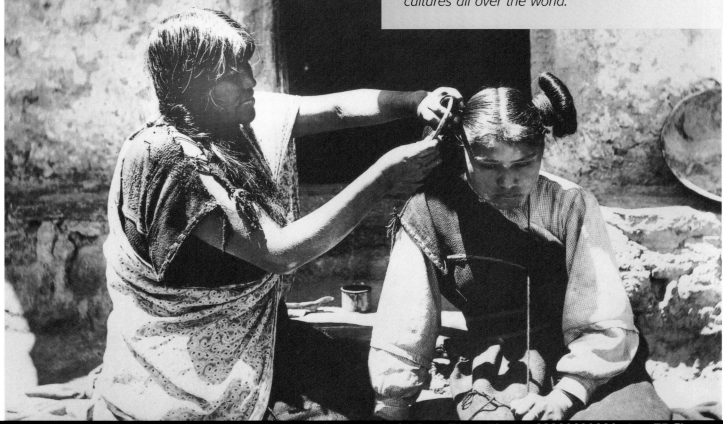

This photograph taken in c.1909 shows a young woman of the Hopi people of Arizona, USA, having her hair dressed. Her hair is in this distinctive style to show that she is unmarried, and looking for a husband. Distinct hairstyles to indicate a person's status or availability for marriage are common in totally separate cultures all over the world.

Central and Southern America

Further south, the styles of Central and Southern America were just as varied. In Central America in the 15th and 16th centuries, Aztec priests wore their hair long and wild. This was to symbolize their association with the forces of nature which they tried to control with human sacrifices.

In Brazil, some of the native people of the Amazon rainforest grow their hair long over their shoulders, but shave their foreheads. Some peoples shave their heads completely, or have a **tonsure** (shaved circle) at the top of the head. This is thought to be a symbolic link with the Moon, which is worshipped by some **Amerindian** people.

FACT

Traditional styles of braids and coloured beads, once worn by women of the Aztec nation, can still be seen in Mexican cities today.

PUDDING BOWL

The people of the Xingu National Park in Brazil cut their hair in a pudding bowl style. Then they coat the head in red pigment that they smooth over the hair using a piece of string held taut between the fingers. Occasionally, additional designs are drawn on top of this red pigment, using black paints.

This Mexican street seller sports a hair style of two side plaits, taken from a central parting. This hairstyle has been worn by Native American women for centuries.

THE MOHAWK

The most famous cut from North America to survive into the 21st century is probably the Mohawk or Mohican haircut. This was first adopted by warriors of the Iroquois people. Achieving this distinctive style was very time-consuming. Sometimes though, animal fur was used instead of real hair. The fur or hair would be held in place with either a metal frame or basketry. In a classic example of people today borrowing directly from historical styles, it has since been taken up by US Paratroopers and punk rockers. It was even worn by footballer David Beckham in the summer of 2002.

FROM WIGS TO HAIR EXTENSIONS

Comings and goings

Throughout European history, a bewildering number of new hairstyles have come and gone. Styles, often first worn by the king or queen, would appear, become popular and spread to other nations. Short hair would be followed by long hair, a clean-shaven face by an elaborate beard and moustache. In **medieval** times a plucked, high forehead was thought to look elegant on women, and was intended to give the illusion of extra height. This style has cropped up totally independently all over the world; for example, the **Amerindians** of the Amazon shave their foreheads.

Hair adornments such as wimples (a piece of cloth draped over the head), veils, curls, waves, pleats, plaits, **braids** – all have come and gone and come in again. When the French King Louis XIV (1638–1715) began wearing a wig because he was going bald, he began a trend for hairpieces that lasted for the best part of two centuries.

Wig's the word

Wigs have been worn in many different cultures – from the nobles of ancient Egypt to the **geishas** of Japan. They were immensely popular in Europe from the 17th to late 18th century, with particular types being worn by particular professions. Judges, coachmen, tradesmen, doctors, army and navy officers all had a distinctly recognizable wig. The fashion for wigs reached a peak in the years before the **French Revolution** at the end of the 18th century. Both women and men wore huge high wigs, which were often full of lice and even rats. Some women's wigs were so large they could be decorated with flowers that were placed inside their own bowl of water – completely hidden inside the wig – to keep them fresh! The style for huge wigs was so popular in London that the main entrance to St Paul's Cathedral had to be raised to allow worshippers to come and go. Wig-making was a huge industry, and poorer people could make money by selling their own hair to wigmakers.

This engraving makes fun of the extraordinary wigs worn by women of the French Court, in the years leading up to the French Revolution in 1789. The upheaval of the Revolution brought about a more sober style of both hair and clothing.

Wigs today

Throughout the 20th century, many women's styles have demanded the use of hairpieces to get the desired look. The 'beehive' look of the 1960s, for example, used hairpieces. **Hair extensions** are popular today and are really just an advanced sort of wig.

This girl is having hair extensions added by her hairdresser. The gun shown contains bonding material so the extensions stick to the hair. Extensions generally last from three to four months.

HAIR AND OUTRAGE

Whatever the period in history, there were always people determined to push the boundaries of acceptable fashion as far as they would go. Looking outrageous is a way of rebelling and of asserting your individuality. In 18th century Britain, young male **aristocrats**, nicknamed Macaronis, wore gigantic wigs and affected **effeminate** clothes and gestures. In Britain in the 1980s, so-called New Romantics (shown here) wore similarly **foppish** clothing and radical **asymmetrical** or brightly coloured hair. Curiously though, by the late 20th century, looking outrageous depended far more on how different you were prepared to look than how much you could afford it.

Hair treatments

From natural to fashionable

There are many different types and colours of hair. At different times, some have been regarded as more attractive than others, but fashion changes all the time. Because of this, the treatment of hair, changing it from natural to something more fashionable, has become as much a part of the hairdresser's art as cutting.

Curly or straight?

Throughout history, curly hair has often been regarded as attractive, even in countries where naturally curly hair is extremely rare. The hair of people from the Indian subcontinent, for example, is not often curly. Women from the South of India would shape their hair into curls and then cover their head in hot mud. When the mud dried, it would be carefully peeled off, leaving a head full of luscious, black curls. This technique was also practised by the ancient Egyptians, who would wind their hair on wooden sticks, cover it with mud, and bake it in the sun. Today the same effect can be achieved much more easily with plastic rollers and an electrical hairdryer. Hairdressers use setting solutions to permanently alter straight hair to wavy or curly hair (a 'perm'). Those with curly hair can even have their hair straightened with perms or **relaxers** designed for the job.

To dye for

Dyeing hair has been practised since ancient times, and often had a terribly unhealthy effect on the hair. Dyes made from leeches and vinegar may have darkened the hair, and a chemical called lye may have lightened it, but frequent use of these substances also led to baldness or brittle, lifeless hair. Hair dyes today are much gentler, and can be used with less risk of damage.

Botticelli's depiction of a Greek myth The Birth of Venus *was painted in about 1485. Venus's long blonde hair was thought to be beautiful then and still is in some cultures today.*

KNOW YOUR FOLLICLES!

The average number of hairs or follicles on a person's scalp is between 90,000 and 150,000. Particular hair colours have particular follicle types and each follicle type is a different shape in cross-section. They can determine what type of hair-care products people are most suited to and how well these products work. In general, people of Asian descent or redheads have the least number of follicles on their scalp, where people with blonde hair or of African descent have the most.

This powder is made from crushed leaves of the henna plant. Henna has been used for thousands of years to colour hair and is a natural alternative to hair dyes.

How much colour?

Some dyes, known as temporary rinses, can wash away with one shampoo. These will really only work when they are the same or darker than your natural hair. Tone-on-tone, or semi-permanent, colours last for longer – up to about 24 washes usually. Like wash-in-wash-out colours, they do not contain a bleach, so they only work with the natural colour of your hair or darker. Other dyes, known as permanent tints, permanently change the colour of the hair. These can take your hair to much lighter tones than your natural colour. However, they need to be retouched at the roots at least once a month as your natural colour grows through.

In an effort to catch the attention of press photographers, American singer Pink models an eye-catching rainbow hairstyle at the 2000 Billboard Music Awards.

FACT

In 1970, hair product manufacturer *L'Oréal* had two shades of red in their product range; now they have nearly 20. Rivals Clairol have over 40!

A CENTURY OF STYLES

Cinema idols

In the early part of the 20th century, cinema was even more popular than it is today. Screen stars became fashion icons to the millions who flocked several times a week to watch their films. Actor Clark Gable inspired a million moustaches, and countless young women flocked to have a pageboy cut after seeing Greta Garbo, or have their hair cut to a bob, like Louise Brooks. Fashionable styles changed regularly throughout the century as screen favourites came and went.

THE BOB

One of the most revolutionary European hairstyles of the last century was the bob. This style, where the hair is cut short evenly around the head, was first worn by women in the 1920s – the years immediately after World War I. It was considered shocking at the time because it went against the conventional image of the long haired, feminine woman.

Rock and roll

For the last 50 years, pop music performers have done more than anything else to determine how young people wear their hair. In 1956, Elvis Presley had his first hit. Within weeks he was a global phenomenon, and millions of young men were copying his greased quiff. In the 1960s, the Beatles and the Rolling Stones inspired millions to grow their hair long or in a shaggy, floppy style.

Long hair became the rock-star hairstyle to imitate until punk came along in the late 1970s, and anyone fashionable and rebellious sported a Johnny Rotten-style crop. This was much shorter, but long enough for it to stick up in spiky tufts. It was often dyed in outrageous day-glo colours, such as pink and green.

The pop group Destiny's Child model a collection of different hair styles. Modern styling techniques using colouring, curling, straightening and hair extensions enable men and women with all hair types to wear a surprising number of different styles.

This recent photograph of Japanese teenage girls shows the enduring hairstyles of the punk rock era of the 1970s. Their bright pink and orange hairstyles have been created with the help of a razor.

Today, these styles – and those of all kinds of performers including nu-metal, rap and hip-hop stars – influence the hair of young, fashionable people the world over. Alesha, Sabrina and Su-Elise of R&B group Mis-Teeq, for example, can be seen with hairstyles ranging from long flowing black ringlets to startling bright-red straight hair, experimenting freely with many different styles.

Styles for all

Now we can draw inspiration for our hairstyles from all over the world. From ancient Greece and the plains of America to pop stars and soccer celebrities, hairstyles and trends have crossed all boundaries, cultures and ages – providing us with a rich source for expressing ourselves through our hair.

FURTHER INFORMATION

Tops tips for healthy hair

! The best recipe for healthy hair is a healthy diet. Drink plenty of water (at least eight glasses a day), eat low fat proteins such as fish, cheese and eggs, and plenty of vitamins and minerals.

! Healthy hair needs a good supply of oxygen and nutrients to the hair follicles. Regular exercise makes your heart beat faster and ensures your hair gets all the goodness it needs from your body.

! Do not use too much shampoo when you clean your hair. This will leave it looking lifeless. A dollop the size of a grape is enough for short hair. A dollop the size of a walnut shell is enough for long hair.

! Do not forget to change your shampoo from time to time, as your hair builds up a resistance to ingredients in a particular shampoo.

! If you are considering dyeing your hair, check how it reacts to a hair colourant by doing a 'strand test'. Apply the colourant to a lock of hair which is usually hidden by a top layer of hair. Then leave it on for the recommended time, and see if you are happy with how it looks.

! Some hair treatment products, such as colourants, can produce a bad reaction on the skin. Before you use a new product, always dab a little of it on the skin on the inside of your elbow. If this starts to itch or turns red, then you should not use this product.

Books

Hair – A Book of Braiding and Styles, Anne Akers Johnson (Klutz Press, 1996)

The History of Hair – Fashion and Fantasy Down the Ages, Robin Bryer (Philip Wilson Publishers, 2000)

The Usborne Book of Hair, Philippa Wingate (Usborne Publishing, 1999)

Websites

http://www.cite-sciences.fr/english/ala_cite/expo/tempo/cheveu/index.html

http://www.costumegallery.com/hairstyles.htm

http://www.beautyworlds.com/hairstylesnf.htm

These sites will be useful for anyone interested in further information on hair-care and hairstyles.

Places to visit

Costume museums may have exhibitions relating to hairstyles and decoration from time to time, and so will other regional museums. Check your local newspaper for listings, or look in the national listing pages of daily newspapers, which often have this information on Saturdays.

GLOSSARY

Amerindian   another word for a Native American

anti-establishment   something which goes against the governing force

archaeologist   person who studies the human and material remains of past civilizations

aristocrats   broadly speaking, the ruling class in a society

asymmetrical   not symmetrical, unbalanced

Barbarian   abusive term for a primitive, brutal people

Beatnik   youth movement from the 1950s characterized by unconventional attitudes, long hair and scruffy clothes

braid   to interweave strands of hair into a plait

buff   dull yellow colour

bust   marble sculpture of a head

Communist   used to describe communism, a form of government where the state controls all property, wealth and industrial production

decadent   indulgent, corrupt ideas or behaviour

dynasty   family who rule a country generation after generation

effeminate   feminine in appearance or behaviour

emollient   substance which has a softening or soothing effect

ethnic   relating to a group of people who share things such as language, culture or religion

Fascist   ultra-right wing political viewpoint or group

fez   brimless, cone-shaped hat

figurines   small pottery or metal figures of people or animals

foppish   overly concerned with fashion or appearance to the point of being ridiculous, especially said of men

French Revolution   drastic upheaval in France, beginning in 1789, when the French monarchy was overthrown

frieze   part of a wall decorated with painted illustrations or sculptures

geisha   Japanese woman who entertains men for a fee. Geishas have highly distinctive hair, make up and costumes.

hair extensions   additional real or synthetic hair, which is woven into a person's hair

Hare Krishna   branch of the Hindu faith devoted to the god Krishna

henna   plant that releases a red pigment from its leaves and stalks

Hindu   person following the religion of Hinduism, which is popular in India and South-east Asia

hippie   youth movement from the 1960s and onwards, characterized by the wish to 'drop out' or live outside conventional society

indigenous   belonging to a place. For example the Australian Aboriginal people are indigenous to Australia.

Islam   one of the world's biggest religions

Judaism   culture and tradition of the Jewish religion

materialism   desire for money and possessions at the expense of all other things

medieval   time period stretching from approximately AD 500 to 1500

migration   movement of people from one part of the world to another

mosaic   intricate pattern or picture made with stones, glass or jewels

mourning   process of grieving for a person who is dead

Muslim   follower of Islam, one of the world's biggest religions

Native American   inhabitant of North or South America before the arrival of Europeans

Orthodox Jew   branch of the Jewish faith characterized by strict observance of Jewish laws

pigment   another name for colour or dye

psychological   relating to psychology, a science concerned with human behaviour

psychologist   scientist who studies human behaviour

puritanical   disapproving of frivolity or luxury

recruit   new member of an organization, such as an army

regime   particular government, such as the Communist regime

relaxer   chemical used on hair to straighten it

relief   form of sculpture where figures are projected from a flat background to give them a three dimensional appearance

rite of passage   ceremony performed to mark a particular stage of someone's life, such as reaching puberty or getting married

sidelocks   long curls at side of head

Sikh   person following the religion of Sikhism

Sikhism   culture and tradition of the Sikh religion

singe   regarding hair, to stop it growing by applying heat to the root

Spartan   from the city of Sparta in ancient Greece

status   the standing or level of respect that a person has in their society

tonsure   distinctive hairstyle, often worn by monks, where the hair is shaved at the top of the head

Tsar   Russian king

turban   cloth that is wrapped tightly around the head covering the hair

visual record   picture, statue or painting, that gives us information about the culture that produced it

INDEX

Titles in the *Body Art* series are:

Hardback   0 431 17923 9

Hardback   0 431 17925 5

Hardback   0 431 17924 7

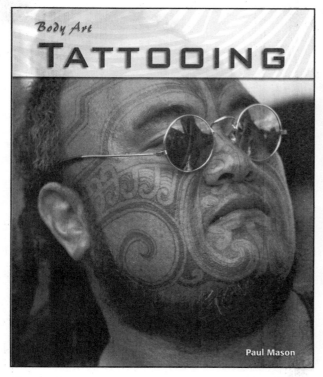

Hardback   0 431 17922 0

Find out about other series by Heinemann Library on our website www.heinemann.co.uk/library

Hereward College

LEARNING RESOURCES
CENTRE